I0830074

Manpower For Manholes!

A Treatise on Truth from Both Sides

Du

ISBN (Paperback) : 978-1-79487-146-5 (Lulu-assigned)

Imprint: Independently published

Categories:

Nonfiction > Social Science > Men's Studies

Nonfiction > Social Science > Gay Studies

Proposed Classifications:

Nonfiction > Philosophy > Actionist

Nonfiction > Culture > Standards

Assfuck it to their face!

If only those with the balls

To do it

SEEING IS STANDING

About the Author

Du is now, by Deed Poll, my legal name, since October 2002. Late 2020, turning 70.

Schizophrenic by professional qualification, free man by occupation, actionist by habit, happy by orientation, dreamer by choice.

NOT so easily fooled by this little world, and its story, I write and self-publish, poetry, books for fun, for a hobby.

Preface

"Assfuck it to their face!
If only those with the balls
To do it

SEEING IS STANDING"

What to do, when society doesn't have legitimate grounds to suppress the assfucking sex among the men, the manfucking men's men?

But, here I give the picture from the other side as well, that based on the "fidelity factor", as given in this exposé, this philosophical and actionistical treatise on Truth from both sides.

I'm still of the mind the situation in present society in this world calls for "assfucking it to their face".

You be the judge.

Manpower For Manholes!

A Treatise on Truth from Both Sides

"I've looked at clouds from both sides now

From up and down and still somehow

It's clouds' illusions I recall

I really don't know clouds at all"

Now see. At First Class, you never say "fuck" to Company, let alone assfuck it to their face.

And all because of the fidelity factor.

The fidelity factor is this: At First Class, you are NOT allowed to touch anybody corporeally except Partner, under pain of worse than Hell forever, for some cold comforts, simplistically put.

"Corporeal" refers to the Corpus, the permanent body, as against "physical", which refers to the Physicus, the assfucking physical bodies that filter incessantly in and out of the Corpus.

The Physicus consists of these assfucking physical bodies, all prime-quality manforms, but like my father the MC said: "No one there."

At First Class, when you meet up with Company, you always see him/them only at eye level, NEVER below the waist, or you will be cutting him/them.

And you always show up in Company riding as ONE manform with Partner.

Now you would be right to
ask: Just how are you going
to do that all the time?

Wouldn't it be stilted and
stiff to carry on so,
routinely as a normal part
of Life?

Won't your eyeballs get
locked up rigid, like in
rigors mortis, for example?

Couple that with: Perish the
notion is too late, the
thought occurs to mind is
too late.

The slightest notion of even just slighting Partner and it's all too late.

Under pain of worse than Hell forever, for some cold comforts, simplistically put.

Like my father the MC said: "Jenseits [YEN-zytes] (That Side, beyond, yonder, yonsides, Jenseits) never so weak-minded. That's all we can say. Too weak-minded to put it any better."

Diesseits [DEES-zytes] (This Side), my father the MC simply said: "Shadow-boxing."

So, how are you ever going to ensure that any thought NEVER EVER occurs to mind?

You'll have to have the resources and ability to take in all of Life, all the World, all Forever, and all, to

accomplish that and have
that as a matter of course
and simple fact of Life.

Like my father the MC said:
"Jenseits, that's where you
really are. Diesseits, you
are just a shadow of
yourself. Anything that
makes you unhappy can't
be."

So, simply put, how Jenseits, "never so weak-minded", carries on, especially at First Class, is just way beyond us Diesseits, where "you are just a shadow of yourself".

But, just the same, even Jenseits, at Lower Classes, I see, especially at Third Class, Company rounds, -- where you get around assfucking with Company.

NOT corporeally, but physically.

As new life manform individual digits, far, far from the First Class Corpus, the corporeal permanent body.

In Lower Classes, where you have the new life meant to be, you have a new generation every new day.

At the end of each new day, -- "Im Herzen, alles gut und KLAR doch schon" ("In the heart, all good and CLEAR already indeed").

So, even Jenseits, there would be a time and place, -- at Lower Classes when doing Company rounds, -- where and when you would be plain and forthright with even Company, who would agree with and even be erfreut (a-joyed) at the prospect of "assfucking it to their face".

But then, even just Diesseits, where "you are just a shadow of yourself", when, for example, a gay couple invites you to their house, you would NOT want to even say the word "fuck" in their presence, let alone "assfuck it to their face".

It is NOT just decorum or polite behaviour.

Rather, because it is premised directly on the fidelity factor, from Jenseits, First Class, and all, it would be an offence against Love, and even an offence against Truth, if you recklessly chose to disregard their Partnership, and all that goes with it, including their inviolable status of that state.

Outside of such direct situations, especially in

Lower Classes settings, in the World, in the Ocean, as far as Du [doo] (you, -- singular), -- the one word to it all, where English just says "Life", -- goes, every man or manform would like nothing better than assfuck manforms and see assfucking manforms assfucking assfucking manforms, in fact nonstop, like breathing out and breathing in.

And so, "assfuck it to their face" would only mean, to Du, and the countless manforms Du includes, -- "SEEING IS STANDING".

And nobody, nothing will get hurt or offended.

NOT Company, Partner, Self, Love, and or Truth, and or anybody and or anything gut und heil (good and hale).

In the mess, especially in these immediate quarters, Diesseits, it is, at least sometimes, hard to tell whether the setting one is in is First Class or Lower Classes.

Oftentimes, it's all jambalaya and mixed up.

You don't have to be in the Corpus, the First Class corporeal permanent body.

The "lines" that come down and around will already mark you out to be in the First Class "mode", or the person and or thing you are with to be "Partner getting around".

And as I always say, -- "Watch the Partner lines."

Where the objection arises is where PAWLITE society, in

this world for example, would castrate and or prevent the use of the word "fuck" in general settings.

All in the name of an artificial, untruthful and unhealthful civility that bears no relation the abovementioned fidelity factor, but imposed on all and sundry to get even robust grown men to be "nice" and ladylike, even among robust grown men.

Where even the Mermaid of Copenhagen is banned from Facebook because of it rules on nudity, as BBC has just in January 2020 reported, even my younger brother, Dom, the heterosexual homogenius, can see it is sick and sickening.

"Truth will out," as English says.

And, as Saint Paul said, --
"The truth will set you
free."

In the army, for example,
especially among the rank
and file, "fuck" gets to be
practically every third word.

Army discipline does NOT
call for an assfucking orgy
every minute of the day, of
course.

But, it is unhelpful and illicit to castrate the men, verbally and or sexually, where and when the assfucking sex is due.

Where, therefore, the assfucking sex is, violently and or insidiously, repressed, suppressed and or outright castrated from

society at large, it behoves
one well to let fly and
indeed call for those with
the balls to "assfuck it to
their face".

Assfuck it to their face!

If only those with the balls

To do it

Pious me!

SEEING IS STANDING